THE MOURNING AFTER

How To Manage Grief Wisely

by
Stanley P. Cornils

PUBLISHED BY
R&E PUBLISHERS
P.O. BOX 2008
SARATOGA, CALIFORNIA 95070
408-866-6303

Typesetting by
STELLA KREBS

Cover by
KAYE DESIGNS

Library of Congress Card Catalog Number
89-64454

I.S.B.N.
0-88247-844-3

INTRODUCTION

In this booklet we shall be thinking primarily of grief as a result of the loss of a loved one by death. As we discuss what we believe to be the better ways of handling the problem, we must bear in mind that the same techniques we mention here would be applicable to a greater or lesser degree in any situation of separation.

When a significant person in your life is removed, you may feel like you have crash-landed into a whole new world. Your feelings of loss and bewilderment will last for a long time. As you make your way through this "valley of the shadow", grief may so completely take over and manage your life that you may feel like a small boat adrift and helpless on a stormy sea. If you do not find some constructive ways of managing it — it will manage you. This is not something that someone else can do for you; grief work is a "do-it-yourself" kind of assignment–painful though it may be.

The purpose of this book is to help you understand what is happening to you, why you feel the way you do, and why you sometimes might be tempted to believe that you are losing your mind. Here we shall attempt to define the meaning and purpose of grief — one's reactions to it — and the most creative ways of handling it.

If you are in the first and acute stage of grief at the time you are introduced to this book, you will, no doubt, feel little interest in reading anything because your power of concentration is greatly lessened. However, may we suggest that you scan the table of contents and then begin reading at any point that seems to speak to your need.

Stanley P. Cornils

Pastor Emeritus
First Baptist Church
Vallejo, California

TABLE OF CONTENTS

THERE IS HELP FOR YOUR GRIEF

If you have recently lost your spouse, a child, or a precious friend in death, you probably feel devastated and that you will never again be happy. Your world has been turned upside down and inside out and you may have lost all interest in everything around you. This is normal. It is true you will never get over it, but you CAN get through it so that your life can again move on.

None of us can prevent what life brings to us, but we can determine what we do about it. There is no experience of life which we cannot work our way through. For every human problem there is a solution, even if it's only learning how to live with the problem. That's what this book is all about.

Grieving the loss of another person is the most basic and painful of all human experiences. It produces a variety of emotional and physical symptoms which are disturbing and sometimes terrifying, mostly because we feel alone and that no one else is suffering as we are.

In a sense, time heals all wounds, but not always in the best way. A broken arm can heal without benefit of medical attention, however, if the broken parts have not been properly aligned, set, and them immobilized in a cast for several weeks, the arm may heal crooked or a joint may not function. The form of the limb will be marred and its usefulness impaired and diminished.

THERE IS HELP FOR YOUR GRIEF! Most of it is at the end of your arm; you have to do it yourself. It is not going to go away by itself; you have to work at it, and this, while you are not highly motivated to do anything. This "laziness of grief" is also normal for most people.

John James, in *THE GRIEF RECOVERY HAND-BOOK,* states, "No book or counselor, or friend or support group can recover you from your grief. Only you can recover yourself." No one drowns just because they fall into the water. They drown because they stay there and don't or won't fight back to save themselves.

If we are aware of the mistakes we might make along the pathway to recovery and how to avoid them, and if we do the necessary grief work and properly carry out the tasks of mourning, the bereavement we suffer today may be a positive help in adjusting and growing in the years ahead. It was Helen Keller who said, "When one door closes, another opens, but often we look so long at the closed door that we do not see the one which has opened for us."

Count your blessings, not your burdens. While you may grieve because of your loss, you can keep yourself from losing all perspective and appreciation for the many good things that can still happen in your life. Make a list of all the people left in the world whom you love and who love you. They can be a help to you. The three greatest sources of help are family, faith, and friends.

THERE IS HELP FOR YOUR GRIEF by ventilating your feelings as you talk with friends and relatives who themselves have walked the road you are now traveling.

You will also discover that most grieving people have the same sort of problems in dealing with their grief.

THERE IS HELP FOR YOUR GRIEF in reading good books related to grief, bereavement, widows and widowers, etc. Our public libraries have scores of excellent volumes on these and related topics. Right now your comprehension span may be very limited and you may feel you are too confused and mixed up to profit from any such exercise. Try it anyway for a few minutes at a time. Pick up a good book, glance through the table of contents until you find some listing that might interest you, and then read it.

It might be necessary to go over it several times. Then think about it often in the hours that follow. Your ability to concentrate will improve as times goes on and you will happen onto things which will help you. Remember, this "grief work" is something no one else can do for you; you have to do it yourself.

THERE IS HELP FOR YOUR GRIEF in becoming a part of a support group made up of people who are engaged in the same struggle you are. They really know how you feel. Find the support groups in your area and decide which one seems right for you, and attend a time or two to get the feel of the group before you join. Don't wait. Take a step, something good may happen. If you don't take a step, nothing will happen. Once you become a part of such a group, you will be gratified by the feelings of caring and support that will be yours. Having such a focus outside yourself will enable you to survive.

There are no magic pills to help you escape the suffering of grief any more than there is an escape from the pain that follows surgery or a severe illness. But you can do more than survive. You can emerge as a better person if you will really work at it. *The worst thing you can do right now is to do nothing.*

> **COURAGE IS NOT HAVING THE STRENGTH TO GO ON; IT'S GOING ON WHEN YOU DON'T HAVE THE STRENGTH.**

Comparatively speaking, there are few experiences in life which we cannot work our way through, if we will only try and keep trying. I firmly believe that you will never meet anything you cannot handle. You may not believe this now, but if you will apply all of the resources available to you, including those within yourself, you will discover strengths you didn't know existed.

If you are willing to work your way through, there can be an end to the sorrow and hopelessness. It is not what happens to you, but what you do about it that determines the ultimate outcome. Happiness depends more on ourselves than on the circumstances of our lives. You cannot control what comes to you, but you can control what you do about it.

How long does all this take? It depends on how well and completely you work at it. Take it a day at a time and in six months some things will have taken a turn for the better, and more will follow in a year, and still more in two years. By that time you will be well on your way toward acceptance, readjustment and recovery. You will never get over your loss, but you CAN get through it.

WE MUST FACE IT

Eventually sorrow finds its way into the lives of most of us. It is unlikely that we can go through life without somewhere, sometime, passing through an experience of grief. Frequently, grief is associated with the loss of a loved one in death, but it is not necessarily limited to bereavement. Grief may come as a result of many other circumstances; it may come when a member of the family goes into the armed forces or away to school; it may be the result of separation during times of war; or it may come to a father or mother when a child goes out into the world to make his own way. Irrespective of its cause, grief is an emotional pain that everyone must face.

Death rides beside us every day. It is a universal experience. In our world, everything that lives will ultimately die; hence, we should be mindful of the possibility of death and include it in our philosophy of life. To face reality is a part of wisdom. It is said that Louis XV of France decreed that the word "death" should never be spoken in his presence, and that everything that might remind him of it be removed from his sight. Refusal to face up to a problem does not nullify the problem, nor does it make it go away.

Bereavement is not a unique phenomenon; it comes to all of us. If we have recently lost a loved one, the experience is new only to us. In the midst of our feelings of bewilderment and loss, we might find it helpful to remember that since time began millions have lived through the experience victoriously.

> **THE MORE WE BECOME ACQUAINTED WITH AND UNDERSTAND THE PROCESSES OF GRIEF, THE BETTER WE WILL BE ABLE TO COPE WITH IT.**

Just as a physician follows well defined and accepted techniques in restoring vital organs to wholeness and health, we all need to follow some basic rules in the control and management of grief. Now is the time to stop to take inventory of what is going on inside us. Unfortunately, death and grief may embarrass some of us who have had so little experience with it that we neither understand it nor know how to respond to it. Perhaps, because we have had so little experience with death, we have no criteria for knowing whether or not our responses are natural and normal. Under most circumstances, a physician can chart the course of convalescence and recovery following surgery. He tells us that the first few days following surgery we will be very aware of pain and may care very little whether "school keeps" or not. However, he assures us that after a week or ten days, we shall be able to return home and that after a few more weeks we can return to work, and ultimately be completely well. The physician's insight encourages us to bear the discomfort an hour at a time as we progress toward complete recovery. Through the physician's help, we understand what is happening to us, and we come to know what is normal, and are better able to bear up under the temporary discomfort.

> **YOU CANNOT CONTROL WHAT LIFE BRINGS TO YOU, BUT YOU CAN CONTROL WHAT YOU DO ABOUT IT.**

It is natural for us to avoid pain; nevertheless, there are many painful experiences that may come to us in the course of our lifetime. We may not be able to prevent their coming, but as creative personalities we have it within our power to determine what these experiences will do to us and how we will cope with them when they do come. We must decide how we will interpret them. Will we look upon the incident as a period of a sentence, a sign of termination that brings life to an abrupt halt? Will we regard death as a semicolon which indicates a change in direction, or will we look upon it as a colon which precedes an explanation or indicates a pause? The choice of interpretation rests with us and with us alone! We need an emotional strategy that will help us manage bereavement positively rather than negatively. The better part of wisdom in dealing with grief would be to *admit to its presence*, accept it as a reality, and then set about to discover the proper technique for dealing with it.

Students of psychology have demonstrated that there are resources within us and available to us that enable us to recover from such traumatic experiences as bereavement. Most grief reactions eventually diminish in severity of and by themselves. That lessening of grief does not mean that we will ever get to the point where the sense of bereavement will cease to be; the feeling of loss will always be with us. But it is also true that there are forces and powers within us that enable us to meet and act upon the conflicts of life in a creative manner.

Not what happens to us, but how we deal with situations will determine the end result. If life throws a dagger at us, there are two ways of catching it: either by the blade or by the handle. When the world gave Jesus a cross, He accepted the worst thing that could ever happen to a man and transformed it into the greatest victory that has occurred in the world. He did not just bear the cross; He used it! And in so doing, He made it a symbol of glory and honor and victory with which we decorate our heroes. Grief does not have to run like a prairie fire out of control; it can and ought to be intelligently managed.

> **SOME PROBLEMS ARE UNSOLVABLE,**
> **BUT CAN BE MADE MANAGEABLE.**

The beauty and opalescence of the pearl presents an object lesson in the proper handling of a difficulty. A cultured pearl is formed by removing a young oyster from the sea and placing within its shell a tiny grain of sand or small pebble. The oyster is then returned to the ocean floor. No one can doubt that the oyster is irritated by this foreign substance within its body, but because it is powerless to get rid of it, it does something else. Hour by hour, day by day, and year by year, the oyster envelops the foreign body with an iridescent film which gradually becomes as hard as stone. This is how a pearl comes into being. Years later the oyster is retrieved and the beautiful pearl is harvested.

The experiences of life come to all of us, much as raw material goes into a factory, and the finished product that comes out on the loading dock is the result of the skill and effort of the craftsmen within the factory. We may see the same principle at work as we watch two small children on the floor playing with similar sets of blocks. One may construct something of childish beauty or interesting intricacy, while the other may fashion something crude or clumsy, or maybe nothing at all. Like the workers in the factory and the children playing on the floor, we largely determine the end result.

This principle might best be illustrated by the Oriental story of Yussef and Ahmed, two young men who day after day sat weaving at their looms. Each morning they were given a supply of yarn for the day, brilliantly colored to represent the galaxy of human emotions. There were many colors among the skeins of yarn. One day there was delivered to both of them a large heap of the black yarn of Sorrow. Yussef was discouraged by such a stark color and he wove the yarn into his pattern in harsh patches. On the other hand, Ahmed used his allotment of black yarn differently and wove it into his design with understanding Sympathy. There were golden threads of Happiness, purple threads of Pain, and blue threads of Discouragement. Yussef did not bother to use many of them. The colors he did choose he shot with bitterness into his pattern. With bold artistry, Ahmed skillfully blended his allotment of precious threads with care and tenderness into the pattern as he wove. When the Master came to inspect their tapestries, Yussef growled that he had not been given the proper yarn; his tapestry was mediocre, almost worthless. But when the Master examined Ahmed's work, he found it a masterpiece of the weaver's art. Ahmed had mingled light with shadow. Then the Master gently said to the two craftsmen, "Both of you had the same materials and you used them as you wished. It is not what comes to your life that determines the pattern, but the use you make of it."

If we react to sorrow in a positive and creative way, it may bring a whole new dimension to our lives. A diamond has may facets and so has a life. Eyes that have never known tears may lack genuine tenderness. The heart that has never been torn by anguish from the loss of a loved one has never sounded its own depths. Only as grief enters into and becomes blended with other elements of our personalities can we emerge as full and mature persons. We grow strong through storm and conflict. Someone has suggested that we never "are"; we are always "becoming". We are the unfinished masters of an unfinished world. After the experience of mourning has run its course, there will be wounds that still ache, there will be losses still hard to bear; but no matter how we may feel about the sorrow itself, most of us would be unwilling to surrender what it has brought and taught us, and we would be reluctant to go back to being the kind of persons we were before the sorrow came to us. The softening, hallowing touch of grief leaves its indelible mark upon our personalities.

GRIEF IS AN EMOTION

Grief is a many-faceted, complex of emotions. It involves our deepest feelings, and as with any other emotion that we may experience, we must decide how we will meet and manage it. We may deny it, we may delay it, we may repress it, or we may accept it and express it as best we can.

What really happens when we react properly to an emotion? How do we control it positively? Every emotion calls for action; the emotion of anger often results in a desire to retaliate; the emotion of love needs the opportunity to express itself; the emotion of fear may cause us to run. Fortunately, most of our emotional episodes provide us with opportunities for action and for understanding the source and cause of the emotion. The emotion of grief, however, is not always so simple to deal with because we can do nothing about the loss which brought it on, namely, the death of a loved one. Death is one messenger to whom we cannot talk back.

Emotions are very real, and we must deal with them realistically. As with any other emotion, we may force grief out of our consciousness through denial or delay. We may not admit to the loss of a loved one by refusing to think of his death. We may even dispose of the personal effects of our beloved, or discard all pictures and mementos of the life and experiences shared with the deceased in an effort to begin a new mode of life that will help us to become successful in forgetting.

However, the denial of expression to emotion does not necessarily destroy or dissipate it. We may merely push it further into the subconscious mind to be confined much like the steam in a pressure cooker. There, in the subconscious, the emotion may stay until its pressure becomes so strong that it will escape in some disguised form, such as nervous exhaustion or some other debility. Psychological and medical research indicates that various types of neuroses and even physical distress can be traced to an experience of bereavement in which grief was repressed and mishandled. "Keeping your chin up" does not really solve anything finally. In trying to follow such a course, we may be fooled into a false sense of maturity that we do not actually possess. Instead of manifesting a strong expression of faith, we are trying to develop a false sense of peace by short-circuiting our emotional processes.

THE WORK OF MOURNING

Grief is normally resolved by mourning, a process generally referred to as grief work or "the work of mourning." To do this work successfully, we who are bereaved work our way mentally, emotionally, and even physically through the various stages of grief. We shall speak of these stages in the pages following as (1) acceptance, (2) expression, (3) emancipation, and (4) readjustment. The challenge we face is that of learning to accept the reality of the separation and to give up, little by little, our emotional dependence on the object of our grief, the one who no longer can share life with us. Only after this has been completed will our lives resume a normal and meaningful pattern. It is only when we try to skip "the work of mourning" that we get into trouble.

GRIEF WORK – IT HURTS BUT IT WORKS.
IT IS PAINFUL BUT IT PAYS.

Grief work is hard work; it is painful and involves suffering. But much like the pain of childbirth, it is a pain with a purpose; it brings forth something. Although the experience may be very distressing, the work of normal mourning is helpful rather than injurious to the bereaved. At times the process may become so very difficult that we are tempted to retreat from reality. Mourning also involves tension: tension resulting from the physical absence and the very real memories of the presence of the departed. True, the person has left us physically, but he has not gone from our emotions. We are torn between a natural longing for our loved one and a recognition of the fact that he is no longer present as a physical reality.

Our attachment to our loved one will lessen gradually but not effortlessly. Only as we succeed in doing our grief work will we again become free and uninhibited. Unless we do the work of mourning properly, we will remain out of touch with reality and be held in bondage to the lost loved one, and we will be thwarted in our efforts to progress through and beyond the experience.

There is no miraculous way to avoid the pain resulting from a surgical operation or the healing of a broken bone. Neither can we look for or expect a miraculous healing of our grief. We can ill afford to become impatient with the slow pathway of healing that leads from sorrow to renewed serenity. We are foolish to attempt prematurely to telescope these successive stages of recuperation and hope for a miraculous cure. We will suffer pain, poignant grief, empty days, resistance to consolation, and disinterestedness in life in general.

However, if we are courageous and resolute, we will again be able to live as our loved one would have wished us to live, and face life bravely and undismayed instead of being lonely, embittered, and made hollow by self-pity. In our present bewilderment, it might be difficult to realize that this could ever happen to us or that life could ever again be meaningful for us. But let us look around and count our many acquaintances who have triumphed over sorrow. Their victories can also be ours, for it is possible to restore the abnormal to the normal through the healing process involved in doing our grief work.

THE MANIFESTATIONS OF GRIEF

Just as there is a common pattern of symptoms and reactions peculiar to a medical disease, so there is also a pattern of symptoms and reactions experienced by most people in acute grief. These reactions do not necessarily occur immediately following the loss of a loved one. Sometimes they are repressed or delayed; sometimes they are exaggerated; sometimes they are apparently absent.

When anything is as common as death, we assume that the reaction to it will be normal and in most instances, it is. When the blunt fact of bereavement hits, and the announcement is made that death has come, most of us are benumbed and bewildered. This numbing effect is the result of our emotional inability to accept the fact of death in a realistic way. Some of us may become hysterical and suffer emotional and even physical paralysis. We are apt to lose our equilibrium and our traditional patterns of conduct. The world has become dead to us, a dreary wasteland with only grief, loneliness, and despair to possess our souls. The situation does not seem real. We may feel that "this cannot be happening to us; this is all a dream and soon we will awaken to find that it is not real." Because weeping is our first response to pain, tears may be our first reaction to the loss of our loved one. We may weep prolongedly and hysterically.

These initial reactions may last from twenty minutes to several hours, and they should be regarded as surface in nature for they seem to have little bearing on our prospect for future adjustment.

> **LEARN TO MANAGE YOUR GRIEF,
> OR IT WILL MANAGE YOU.**

Our grief will either completely control and manage us, or we will learn to control and manage it. Needless to say, many of us never conquer grief; instead we are conquered by it. If we allow it, grief can and will destroy us. What it does to us will be determined by how we respond to it. Someone has suggested that grief is like a bewitched pogo stick, it will make us jump in some direction, but which way we know not unless we have had previous experience in using it. The child who has spent many hours and experienced many bruises in learning to ride the pogo stick can, ultimately, make it take him where he wants to go. The spectre of our grief can be transfigured, our sorrow can become a sacrament, and we can learn to be victorious over our grief if only we will learn how to control it intelligently.

Because grief is such a painful experience, our natural tendency is to run from it and resort to anything that will help us bypass the pain for the time being. Not infrequently, a physician will prescribe sedatives to help us through the first stages of our grief experience, and such medication may prove to be a real help in our time of great need, but sedatives should be used sparingly and only in situations where there is real mental abnormallity. The normal reaction to loss should run its course and not be suppressed. More often than not, sedation only delays the reaction and the longer "the work of mourning" is delayed, the more difficult it will be to control grief effectively. If we try to circumvent the emotional stress of grief, we may succeed only in delaying the cure. The work of mourning should not be postponed.

> **FOR EVERY HUMAN PROBLEM THERE IS A SOLUTION, EVEN IF IT'S ONLY LEARNING HOW TO LIVE WITH THE PROBLEM.**

Following the initial onset of grief, waves of acute distress may overcome us when we are reminded of the deceased. The throat tightens, we experience a choking sensation and a shortness of breath, we may lack power, we climb a flight of stairs or walk to the corner and feel exhausted, our every activity becomes an effort, we feel a weight on our chest, we may gulp in long, sobbing sighs as though fighting for air, our appetites vanish, our saliva ceases to flow, our food tastes like sawdust, and our bowel and kidney actions may become irregular. Nothing has meaning, everyone seems far away, and nothing seems real. The lights of the heavens seem to have gone out and we feel we are left in desolation and darkness. When someone demonstrates kindness, sympathy, or recalls a sacred memory, we become overwhelmed by our sorrow.

There are still other possible reactions; we may have a feeling of emptiness or of living in a dream, we may become hostile, we may behave in a stiff and formal manner, we may react toward other people with irritation and even anger, we may become obsessed with the mental image of the deceased, we may exhibit complete disinterestedness in our environment, we may deviate from our normal pattern of conduct, we may manifest a disorganized and undependable attitude, we may feel that we are losing our mind, we may want to talk incessantly about the lost one, and we may have a feeling of restlessness as we repeat motions without zest or meaning.

We have little or no capacity to initiate or organize activity, we procrastinate, we may sometimes imitate traits and mannerisms of the deceased, especially those dominant during the last illness, we may imitate a gait or be absorbed by an interest in the things the deceased was interested in, and we may feel an emotional separation from other people and a resentment toward everyone whose life has been undisturbed.

To any of us who are novices to grief, it may seem that such a long list of symptoms and complications is unrealistic. We must remember, however, that in losing our loved one, a part of our larger self has been amputated; life's pattern has been upset; our focus on life has become blurred and until we acquire a new focus, we must accept the fact that our scheme of life may be disorganized.

Almost everyone of us who loses a loved one should expect these reactions. They are all within the range of normalcy. If we understand them and do our "grief work" courageously, we will express rather then repress our emotions by readjusting our attitudes and forming new relationships. In this way, we may discover a true and therapeutic strategy for dealing with our grief. This mental detour does not mean that there will come a day when we will no longer feel our loss, but when we have succeeded in placing limits on our own selfish interest, we shall have gone a long way toward mastering our grief.

ACCEPTANCE

Acceptance is the first link we must forge in the experience of bereavement if we are to deal with it successfully. Although the terminal illness of our loved one may have been lengthy and taxing and death may have been expected for weeks or even months, we are never ready for it when it does come.

Most of us come to realize quite early in our experience of living that we will be spending much of our lives becoming accustomed to things we had not anticipated. Bereavement is one of these things. When the telegraph messenger comes to our door with a message, what do we do? Shut the door in his face, refuse to accept the message, or try to run away? Wisdom suggests that we accept the message because no matter what action we take, we cannot change the content of the message he brings. In real life we would accept the message and act accordingly. So must we accept death, admit to it, and face it as a reality; for if we fail to accept death realistically, we will also fail in handling it intelligently and creatively.

It is not being heroic to continue as though nothing has happened because something *has* happened. We feel we have lost a vital part of ourselves. Trying to escape from reality is not being heroic. We cannot settle anything without settling it aright, and the problem of grief cannot be dealt with correctly and creatively until we have faced it and accepted it. When we dodge or bypass or run away from grief, we find only a temporary refuge, because sooner or later, grief will track us down and we will have to deal with it.

> **"WE MUST NOW ACCEPT THE UNACCEPTABLE AND SURMOUNT THE INSURMOUNTABLE."**
> *Emperor Hirohito upon Japan's surrender*

Psychology offers much evidence to show that personality grows by confronting the conflicts of life positively and constructively rather than by circumventing them. We do not become wholesome, creative individuals by walling ourselves off from our conflicts or by opening gates for a hasty retreat. It is far more therapeutic for us to recognize, face, and conquer the conflicting issues of life. In dealing properly with these conflicts, we discover all the available resources that can contribute to our further growth.

Our social system provides us with many ways of masking the stark reality of death. We refer to our dead loved ones as having "passed away", as "being asleep", or as "having departed". It would be better for us if we were not so afraid of the word "death". Calling it some other name does not solve our problem, nor does such a reference help us to believe "there is no death." The poet's words just quoted are true because they imply life everlasting. Death does not mean extinction. However, physical death is very real.

We would not decry the magnificent artistry of the mortician and the comforting appointments of the

modern funeral home. Funeral directors and their sur-
roundings have done much to lessen the shock of bereavement; but when we regard these as means of denying the
fact of physical death, we are in need of help. Our at-
tempts to disguise the reality of death reflect a desire to
treat death as unreal, as if we could ease the pain of our
loss by denying its reality. This dilemma creates a serious
conflict within us who know the reality of our loss more
keenly than anyone else could ever know it, and yet all
around us so much is being done to deny or disguise it. We
cannot do anything constructive about trouble by refusing
to accept it or by running away from it. In trying to elude
the reality of death, we only harbor and nourish a mood
that may bring us into greater difficulty unless we find a
way to rise above it.

There is an old story of an oak tree and a reed which
grew close to each other on the side of a hill. One day the
wind came with hurricane force, threatening to destroy
them both. The oak stiffened its branches and prepared
to fight, but the reed only quivered in terror. After the
storm had passed, the oak lay uprooted on its side while
the reed, uninjured, soon stood as straight and tall as ever.
When the dying oak asked the reed what made the dif-
ference, the reed replied: "I bent with the wind; I accepted
it."

EXPRESSION OR SUPPRESSION

One of the laws governing human nature holds, in effect, that an emotion, once touched off, ushers in a chain of events within the body which in some way or another must be externalized by some sort of action if the cycle is to be complete. This action – chemical, skeleto-muscular, neural, or mental – will automatically discharge the energy produced by the emotion. The emotional chain is never completed until the appropriate act or its substitute has been performed. For most of us, our first reaction to the death of a loved one gives rise to a feeling of numbness, and even disbelief. But what is to be regarded as normal beyond this point?

We can conclude from studies made in this field that there is only one remedy for grief, and that is to grieve. We should not be ashamed to grieve. We should give vent to grief as we feel it. The ancient Jews had a custom that allowed for a week of mourning, during which the bereaved and his friends were allowed to talk about the deceased and his virtues. This custom was a wise and a healthful one, for there is a close relation between the healing of physical wounds and the healing of emotional wounds. If we are injured, our blood flows freely to cleanse the wound and then to heal it. So it is with our grief. If we allow it to flow freely and thereby purge itself, our emotional wound will heal. But if we distort, conceal, or deny our normal feelings, we provide fertile grounds for a breakdown. We should allow a bleeding heart a clear leeway for its expression of grief. Instead of distracting our attention from our bereavement (a procedure that should come much later in the healing process), we should speak of our loss, talk of our sorrow, and eulogize the beauty and virtues of our departed one.

There are those who object to a display of grief because they fear that such expression may lead to a nervous collapse. Actually, the opposite is true. Normally, we do not come apart at the seams emotionally as a result of expression of nervous or emotional reaction; more often than not a nervous breakdown results from the repression of emotions. The more we express our grief, the better will be our emotional health in the long run. In essence, we get well by suffering.

Many of us who suppress grief may only deceive ourselves and others into thinking that we are thereby overcoming it. We seldom overcome grief so easily for grief does not dissolve by suppression. It merely slips underground where it may produce a psychotic illness or cause subtle and damaging changes to our personalities. When we repress any negative emotion (including grief), the emotion is not necessarily dispelled; it may only be building up to volcanic proportions. When the eruption finally does come, the consequences can be more serious than if we had faced and accommodated rather than repressed our original feelings. Feelings walled up within ourselves mean trouble ahead.

TEARS AND TALK

Tears are important in the nurturing of the spirit, but do we really understand the function and meaning of them? God gave us tears for a purpose. There are few things as comforting and soothing as the consoling effect of quiet tears; for tears have the power to dissolve the many tensions inherent in our experiences with sorrow. Tears, warm and wet, are soothing and can do much to help wash away the irritants of our lives.

TEARS ARE EMOTIONS TURNED LIQUID.

We should not be ashamed of legitimate tears or feel guilty about shedding them. We may discover that we can see farther through a tear than through a telescope. Weeping can be appropriate, noble, and majestic. Our tears can be crystallized into lenses through which we can better see God's purpose for us and our loved one. God washes our eyes with tears so that we may see the otherwise invisible land where tears shall be no more.

Talking about our sorrow also helps release tension and dissolve the pain of the grief experience. It is true that each time we talk about a painful experience, our pain is eased just a little more. It is by speaking to others of our loss and sorrow that we learn to bear pain. Memories of our loved one may continue to come back to us, but their power to hurt will have been dissipated.

Talking also has a therapeutic value. First, it is cathartic. When we verbalize, we help release the pent up tensions resulting from grief. An angry man yells; a terrified woman screams; and a bereaved person sheds tears and talks. Through verbalization our feelings of loss, loneliness, guilt, anger, and hostility toward the departed are brought to the surface of our consciousness where we can deal with them.

In the second place, talking provides us with insight, which enables us to see more clearly our real feelings and problems. We should not be afraid of verbalizing our feelings of anger and hostility toward our loved ones because we should recognize that they too possessed the weaknesses and failings of mankind. Only after we have achieved this insight will we discover that new feelings and reactions will be forthcoming.

In the third place, the talking process establishes a wholesome relationship with the persons in whom we confide. In a very real sense, they help us bear our sorrow by knowing our feelings about it.

A few words of caution should be spoken at this point concerning the expression of our grief. First of all, when the death of a loved one interrupts our normal pattern of life, we may try to cope with our loss by rationalizing. We may attempt to exercise extreme self-control, acting as though nothing had happened. We may see new interests in life and exhibit great bursts of energy and enthusiasm as we become overly busy in our efforts to avoid loneliness and memories. Some of us may try to "cover up" by embarking on some kind of a binge, forgetting that we cannot drink, smoke, work, play, or eat our way out of grief nor find the solution to any of our problems by carrying on any activity solely for escape.

Our second word of caution has to do with a tendency and temptation to syndicate our sorrows. They should not be shared with everyone we meet. We recall the story of a boy who had a sore thumb and who told everyone he met about his hurt as he painfully unwound the bandage before the eyes of all who would listen to his tale of woe. His sore thumb not only dominated his horizon, but also the horizons of all who knew him. Every time they thought of him, they remembered his sore thumb. So with us; how much better it would be for us and our friends if, when they think of us, they would not think of us as being obsessed by sorrow, but as courageously mastering it.

In the third place, we must be careful that the social pressures of our culture do not prohibit us from doing the kind of mourning that will have a therapeutic effect. Our culture has a rather highly developed pattern which our reactions of grief should follow. There are certain established duties required of us who are mourners. We curtail and restrict our social activities and dress somberly in a mode symbolic of the feelings a bereaved person should have. We as mourners may thereby find ourselves between the two horns of a dilemma. On the one hand, we may feel the necessity for the "proper amount of tears" to demonstrate and prove our affection for the departed; and on the other hand, we may try to "bear up wonderfully." Despite the fact that during the past few generations our culture has made much progress in a better direction, it is still necessary for us to remember that by trying to satisfy the social demands for a particular type of mourning (which is usually superficial and has little regard for our true feelings), we may also be substituting this type of surface mourning for the deeper experience of grieving which is really necessary and we may thereby fail to find real and permanent healing. The proper response to our loss will probably be the one that comes most naturally.

The final word of warning has to do with an excessive display of grief. There is a thought-provoking passage in Rabbinic wisdom that says, "It is impossible not to mourn, but to mourn excessively is forbidden." Excessive grief is seldom a genuine way of showing devotion to our departed loved one. Would it please our loved one to see us so completely given over to sorrow that we are beside ourselves to the point where no one can do anything with us or for us? Excessive grief more often than not brings in its wake deterioration of the personality, upset digestion, malfunctioning of the bodily organs, and a general impairment of health.

In the Jewish Talmud, there is a story of a man who had a little girl, his only daughter, who became sick and died. His heart was broken. Despite all the efforts of his friends to comfort him and help him realize that life does go on, he refused to be comforted.

One night he dreamed that he was in heaven and saw little girls in a pageant. Each girl carried a lighted candle. The candle carried by his own daughter was unlit. As he took her in his arms and caressed her, he asked, "Why is your candle not lit?" She answered, "Sometimes it does light, but your tears always put it out."

It is natural for us to be disturbed, heartbroken and concerned when a loved one is taken from us. But to despair over much and to be unwilling to recognize God and the eternal life he gives us is both unwise and unhealthy. The sun always rises to shine through the clouds after the darkest night, but constant tears and lamenting will prevent us from seeing the light.

EMANCIPATION

The third step in doing our grief work involves learning how to free ourselves from the bondage of the physical existence and coexistence with the loved one. This means that we must go over and over the memories of our former associations with the loved one until we are sufficiently emancipated and free to go on and assume new relationships. Unless we do this, we will make little progress and we will be out of vital touch with reality.

Because bereavement is difficult to accept, we attempt to retreat to a magic world of memories dominated by our loved one. We may set an extra place at the table for the deceased as though he were to be present, converse with him at the graveside, or summon his spirit for advice. These are touching evidences of our devotion, but such practices are inadequate substitutes for grief work and may even handicap us in performing our responsibilities to the living and may delay our readjustment to life and possibly threaten our mental and physical health. As long as we try to keep our sorrow alive artificially, it will continue. As long as we use a trick – and we know it is a trick – we are in control of the situation, but when we begin to fool ourselves, the trick is controlling us, and we are in need of help.

We will achieve mental balance if we will courageously accept and live through the pangs of loneliness rather than attempt to evade them. It is true that the melody our loved one played upon the instrument of life will never be played in quite the same manner again, but this fact does not mean that we should close the keyboard and allow the instrument to gather dust. Death has disorganized our scheme of life, and it will remain that way until we develop a new perspective.

Just as mourning is necessary in performing our grief work , so should we allow our memories to help us in our grief work. Our well-meaning friends may avoid references to our loss because they want to help us forget, but forgetting is just what we do not want to do. In making our way through this difficult task, we should go over and over our memories of our beloved until we become emancipated and can accept new relationships within a framework from which our loved one has gone. Although this is a slow and painful process, and may even be accompanied by physical and emotional discomfort, we must face up to it and undertake it honestly and courageously. We may be surprised to discover, in time, that we can again talk about memories and meditate upon them. As we do this, our pain will grow less and we will be able to recall and adjust to additional memories.

It may help us to think of our lives as being a maze through which we and our beloved traveled together for many years. Along the pathway we left a cord to mark our journey. At many turns, we shared experiences which now have become only memories. At one turn our beloved was taken away and we were left standing alone. Are we to go on as though nothing has changed? Common sense tells us we must let our beloved go. But what do we do with all these experiences of the past? Probably the most helpful thing we can do is pick up the cord and retrace our steps and our experiences even to the time and place we began our lives together. Doing so will help us to surrender our loved one and also help us to design a new pattern for our lives, a pattern in which the loved one exists only as a memory. This does not imply that we have forsaken our attachments to our loved one, but rather that we have accepted the idea of living with a memory, yet not being in bondage to it.

Mrs. Joshua Liebman, whose husband wrote *Peace of Mind,* tells of her own experience with grief following her husband's death: "To make myself realize that Joshua was really gone and to try to function in a world without him, I began by doing alone or with Liela [their adopted daughter] the things I had formerly done with Joshua." She continues by telling of the wonderful times she and her husband had had in New York. Shortly after his death, she made her first return trip to these same places abounding in exciting and happy memories for her. She continues: "I took the bitter medicine. I gazed unseeingly into shop windows, dined without appetite at our favorite restaurants, bought tickets for theaters and movies, accepted invitations to the homes of friends. I cannot pretend that I enjoyed myself. I felt like an amputee trying to walk on artificial legs. It would be foolish for me to say that even after eight years I have entirely succeeded in conquering my grief. I still feel, as the poet Heine said, 'a toothache in my heart.' Grief's slow wisdom, I have learned, comes slowly indeed."[1] Painful is the surgery that removes so much of one's life!

So, instead of trying to forget, we should recall our relationships with the departed. We should relive certain of our experiences in memory, think and talk freely of the deceased, and face up to the adjustments that are necessary. Mourning is accompanied by suffering, but by a suffering that promotes healing. Through this kind of grief work, the relationship is truly severed; we set our loved one free and in so doing we also set our own selves free to relate to other persons and objects.

By these rational acceptances, we are transformed and can independently and resourcefully cope with the world of reality without our loved one. At first, we may be unable to tolerate the thought of the everyday occupations and activities that we associate with the departed. However, we must ponder on every object and situation, and foster the association until we can accept our loss unemotionally.

---

[1]*Woman's Home Companion,* September, 1956, pp. 4-6.

READJUSTMENT

Mourning becomes therapeutic when we can face reality, accept our loss, and work out a new organization for living. When death terminates a happy and vital relationship, it is necessary that we find a substitute for the broken relationship. We need to discover new patterns of action and new areas of interest to compensate for the life design interrupted by death.

These substitute patterns do not come spontaneously and effortlessly. In grief, there is no short cut to readjustment and renewed life interest. We never learn to do arithmetic by copying the results from the answer key in the book. We will know many lonely hours and empty days; often we may feel that we can never recapture an interest in human affairs.

> **SELF-PITY IS ONE HUMAN EMOTION**
> **THAT PAYS NO GOOD DIVIDENDS.**

More often than not, our grief will run its course and it will eventually decrease in severity; but if our grief is founded on a vacuum, self-pity will rush in to fill the void and a mind invaded by self-pity may become unsound. An emotional wound free of self-pity will heal normally and quickly, but if it has been infected by self-pity, it may become very difficult to heal.

A very vital part of our readjustment process concerns our renewal of former relationships with other people as soon as possible and our forming and developing new interests in people and activities. The most trying days of our bereavement are not the days preceding the funeral but the first days following it. We who are bereaved evidence a tendency to build a wall around ourselves with our grief and retreat from life's stream of reality. No one individual or group of individuals can bridge the gap left by our loved ones. Friends cannot be expected to take the place of the departed in our lives, but we, as social beings, need the help that friends and the assuming of social responsibilities can give us.

> **IT IS POSSIBLE TO GRIEVE FOR A LOSS AND STILL KEEP YOURSELF FROM LOSING THE PERSPECTIVE AND APPRECIATION FOR THE GOOD THINGS THAT REMAIN IN YOUR LIFE.**

Despite the sudden void created by the death of our dear one, we must consider and be mindful of our devotion and responsibility to the living as well as to the dead. When sorrow overtakes us, we are tempted to drop out of affairs and retreat within ourselves in loneliness. When a rider is thrown from his horse, he must remount as soon as possible if ever he is to ride again. We, too, need to be challenged to live again. We cannot go backwards; we must move ahead. One step, then another, and then another. Activity is a very necessary part of the cure we need. By swinging into action, we can build our bridge to the future because activity is symbolic of life's forward movement. However, we should not be dismayed when we resume our social responsibilities and relationships to find ourselves somewhat unhappy and even uncomfortable in the company of those whom we should enjoy.

> ANY GOOD THAT MAY COME TO YOU IN THE FUTURE
> WILL DEPEND MORE ON YOU THAN
> ON ANYONE ELSE.

Every human being can build new bridges of human companionship throughout his life. This capability is not reserved by youth alone. We, as human beings, possess the ability to weave new patterns of interpersonal relationships that will make us richer, more creative, more interesting and more dynamic individuals. Those of us who have recently undergone surgery have perhaps been surprised and even amazed when our doctor leaves orders for our nurses to get us out of bed as soon as possible, even the day following the operation. Medical scientists have discovered that the sooner an impaired organ can assume normal functioning, the more rapid will be its recovery.

Perhaps we should sound a word of caution here relative to the frequent temptation to make impulsive and radical changes in our way of living in an attempt to "get away from it all." Even though our home or apartment may be for us a storehouse of memories, we should make changes gradually, and then only after we have carefully pondered our reasons for making them. We should exercise similar caution before rushing back to our business too soon after the funeral merely to be absorbed in activity. We do not escape grief by hurrying back to anything! In so doing, we may only submerge our grief deeper within ourselves where it may long remain as an inner tension that could give rise to further complications. Any rushing back to anything may delay the contemplation that we need to help us reach the ultimate and satisfactory answers. Let us follow further the analogy of the surgical operation!

The doctor also knows that unless an organ is given an opportunity to heal properly, his patient may suffer serious consequences as a result of returning to work too soon following surgery. The surgeon knows that the healing of the body takes time. It takes time, too, to recover emotional balance. Bereavement involves our emotions, and the necessity for doing our grief work properly is so urgent that we should consider taking some leave time to permit us to put our emotional house in order.

**YOU WILL NEVER GET OVER YOUR GRIEF,
BUT YOU CAN GET THROUGH IT.**

GUILT FEELINGS

One of the severest ordeals we as bereaved persons may experience concerns our possible feelings of guilt engendered by the death of our loved one. Many of us have guilt feelings relating to the deceased, feelings that may or may not be justified. Any feeling of guilt is disturbing. Regardless of whether our guilt feelings are justified or imagined, they are very real to us, and we must deal with them if we are to find relief.

These guilt feelings arise from our actual or fancied neglect of or wrong-doing toward the deceased. We may scourge ourselves with such thoughts as, "Why did we not take that trip while our loved one was still with us? Should we have called the doctor sooner? Why did we not call in a specialist? Why did we not get our beloved to the hospital sooner? Why had we not been more considerate and thoughtful? Why did we not spend more time with the one who has been taken from us? Why did we make as many demands of the departed? Why didn't we do this or that? If only we could do things over!" These "if only's" are the hallmarks of grief, and too often we assemble them only to fashion a whip of remorse. We need not feel responsible for another person's death. We must not assume too much. To rehearse our own set of "if only's" is like wiggling a sore tooth to make it hurt more. It may have been too late to do anything for the departed love one and in all probability we did our very best. None of us can do more. Be these things as they may, we can find solace in confession and through confession learn that forgiveness awaits us.

UNRESOLVED GUILT CAN LAST A LIFETIME.

ANGER

When we suffer the loss of someone or something precious to us, it is natural and normal, but not necessarily universal, that we protest and become angry at what has happened. We ask WHY? This little word asks a big question and anticipates an answer which might not be forthcoming. Anger is a part of grieving for many people. The pain is so great that we seem to have to blame someone or something: the doctor, the nurses, the hospital, the funeral director, the clergyman, God, ourselves, and even the loved one who has died and left us to deal with all these problems. The person who is now gone would not have caused the death unless that person died of suicide.

We can also be angry at the means of death: the lake in which the loved one drowned, the airplane that crashed or its pilot who made an error, the automobile involved in the accident, the faulty design of the highway, or even the forces of nature. Our anger could include the driver who may have been at fault, or the negligent employer or employee at the workplace.

No matter how much we wish it weren't so, anger is sometimes unavoidable in life. Anger may be involved even in day-to-day relations as we mingle with those we love.

There is no simple solution that will fit everyone. Suffice it to say we should neither ignore anger nor suppress it. Anger is not likely to go away by itself. Usually there is something we can do. For example, if a water supply pipe begins to freeze, and nothing is done about it, the ice within the pipe will expand as it freezes and the pipe will burst. To avoid this, if we can't change the temperature, we open a faucet somewhere in the system which permits the water to flow, ever so slightly. More often than not, this will keep the temperature of the pipe above the freezing level.

One of the first things we should do is to acknowledge that we are angry. This may be difficult for you, and you may feel guilty about admitting that you are angry, and you don't need a guilt trip right now. The fact that you are angry might also be frightening at first. You may ask yourself, "where will this take me? Where will it end? I certainly don't want to hurt someone?" If it is not properly dealt with, it may result in bitterness, which is grief-anger gone hard. These are reasonable considerations. In a real sense, anger is danger without the "D".

Early on it is wise to identify with whom or at what you are angry. If it is a person, go to that person and express your feelings calmly and constructively no matter how difficult it is for you to do so. This will help defuse the anger. If you cannot get to them in person, write them a letter; keep it on your desk a few days and read it several times before you mail it. In doing this you might discover some better ways of saying what you want to say. In this process be sure to ask yourself: "Did this person knowingly and wittingly contribute to the death of my loved one?" The key word in this exercise is forgiveness. Not forgiving will take a heavy physical, mental and spiritual toll on your life. You, rather than the person you are blaming, will pay the most. I believe this is what the Apostle Paul had in mind when he said: "Be ye angry and sin not", Ephesians 4:16. Jesus also spoke about this in Matthew 18:15 and ff: "If thy brother shall trespass against thee, go and tell him his fault between thee and him alone: if he shall hear thee, thou hast gained thy brother."

Norma's father died in his early fifties of natural causes. She was a sincere and consistent Christian and couldn't understand why she had been wrestling with this loss for so many months. One day she confided to her husband that she was really angry with God about her loss. He inquired if she had ever told God about her feelings. She replied that she didn't think it would be proper. Then he asked her, "Do you think God will come unglued if you tell Him how you feel?"

Several days later, she went to the cemetery, stood by her father's grave, looked up to Heaven, and prayed, "God, I'm angry with you for letting this happen to me." She reports that it helped her. This approach is not new. I believe that listening to our anger is one of God's ways of helping us with our healing. After all, isn't He the Wonderful Counselor? Tell Him how badly you feel and ask for His grace in helping you understand and accept it.

Because our loss is so new and the hurt so raw, it might seem that even our dearest friends and loved ones conspire to hurt us. Words that were meant to console only make us more angry. Almost two years after the loss of her husband, Marge one day confided to the members of her support group, "I was so mixed up and was always angry with everyone; it seemed that it was the whole world against Marge. Every night I prayed that I wouldn't wake up the next morning."

Our society doesn't know how to deal with condolences. We haven't been trained in what to say or what not to say. Statements like, "It was God's will," or "I know just how your feel," and "Time will heal," almost always increase the anger already there. Forgive these well meaning friends, for they know not what they do, even though they mean well.

In such situations, it is best to express your appreciation for their concern but also share your feelings about the condolence without turning them off and away from you. At this juncture, you need all the friends you have; you cannot afford to lose any of them. If you persist in venting your anger in all directions, people will soon desert you as they would desert a sinking ship. Most people are uncomfortable in the presence of angry people.

It is more appropriate and beneficial to share your feelings in confidence with understanding friends whom you can trust and who are willing to listen.

Join a support group in your area. Here you will find people in the same circumstances who can share and appreciate your feelings. Within the fellowship of such caring persons you can safely vent your feelings.

In my studies and observations of people, I have come across a great many other things we can do to lower the level and intensity of our anger. Most of them would come under the heading of "safety valves" to keep us from flying completely apart. I don't suggest that you try all of them, but I feel secure in predicting that some will be helpful in defusing anger.

Engage in some sort of strenuous exercise, such as using the exercycle (grip the handles tightly and pedal away until the sweat begins to run down your face), jog or run around the block a time or two, telephone a dear friend, write a letter you should have written a long time ago, vacuum the house, take a warm bath or shower, hammer on the bed with a ball bat or broom handle, clench your fists and beat on a pillow, mow the lawn, play a vigorous game like tennis, soccer, or racquet ball, go bowling with an understanding friend, go shopping with someone and buy a gift for yourself, paint or redecorate a room, do something for someone else, write down your anger on a piece of paper, invite a friend to dinner and spend most of the day cooking, find a place where you can scream and not be heard by anyone else — then scream. One widow suggests listening to John P. Sousa's "Stars and Stripes Forever" with the volume turned up very loud while you go through the appropriate physical motions as an accompaniment.

Lynn Caine in *BEING A WIDOW* said, "Releasing energy on an emotion that you feel is out of control is part of recovery and that is the direction which you want to go."

God has given us the ability to deal with our bodies and emotions, but we must be willing to engage ourselves in the process.

Try it. There is help for your grief, but it's up to you to find it, appreciate it, and make it work for you.

AMBIVALENCE

Contradictory emotions may also be the cause of guilt feelings which accompany grief. These guilt feelings are subtly allied with the feelings of unresolved hostility toward the departed. Nothing human is perfect. All of us experience moods of resentment and hostility even toward our most beloved persons. Our purest and noblest love may sometimes be colored by a tincture of anger. This is true because we are human – and humankind is not perfect.

Some of us may go all the way through our lives without ever admitting to ourselves or to anyone else that we have experienced moods of hatred or resentment toward our loved ones. As a result of such an attitude, many of us who have lost loved ones spend much time in our efforts to adjust to our loss by glorifying and idealizing by thought and word the qualities of the departed. In this way, we unconsciously attempt to resolve the existing guilt feelings. We might say that such purging is our way of paying off an emotional debt..

The free expression of grief is difficult as long as we have any negative feelings toward the departed one. Both education and religion conspire to make us feel guilty of our normal aggressive impulses. Working through these feelings becomes more difficult if we are ashamed, for when we are ashamed, we often attempt to conceal our feelings even from ourselves by repressing our contrition rather than by admitting it to ourselves and others. In order to keep this ambivalence from becoming obvious, we may magnify our love for the departed or protest either too much or too long and so prolong our grief. We are being much wiser when we review our unpleasant as well as pleasant relationships with the deceased. It is entirely proper for us to express our feelings in a legitimate and wholesome manner in every dimension of our lives.

ABNORMAL GRIEF

The majority of grief situations are normal. Most of us meet the crisis situations of life with enough strength of personality and momentum to get through them with a capacity we did not know we possessed. However, our grief can become morbid and abnormal when we cannot bridge the gap made by broken relationships and find comfort and solace from new ones.

> **IT IS IMPOSSIBLE NOT TO MOURN;**
> **BUT TO MOURN EXCESSIVELY IS FORBIDDEN.**
> *The Talmud*

Our morbid grief reactions are distortions of natural grief. There are two types of abnormal grief; the first is evidenced by a delay of reaction. Should the bereavement occur at a time when we are confronted with important tasks and the necessity for maintaining the morale of others, we may exhibit little or no reaction for weeks or even much longer. We delay the grieving period, but we cannot do so indefinitely.

If we do not grieve at the time of our loss, grief will come later and perhaps at a greater cost to our whole personality. Upon the death of our beloved and for a short period afterwards, we may appear calm and composed. Later, however, we become more aware of the reaction of grief. Sometimes this delayed reaction occurs when we are near the age of the recently deceased. In most instances, this delayed reaction may be attributed to our lack of experience with bereavement.

Studies made on the effect of grief indicate that a repression of emotions arising from bereavement is later apt to result in morbid reactions. Some folk become enraged and angry with the whole world without really knowing why. Others suffer a severe depression for many years following the loss of a loved one without being aware of any relation between their continued depression and the denial of their grief.

The second type of morbid reaction to bereavement that we may experience involves a change in our conduct. We may indulge in motiveless activity; we may evidence symptoms characteristic of the illness of the deceased; we may encourage and even develop psychosomatic conditions, such as rheumatoid arthritis, or asthma; we may obviously exhibit an unusual attitude toward our friends and relatives. We may feel irritable, not want to be bothered, avoid social activities, and be afraid we might alienate our friends by our lack of interest and our hypercritical attitudes. Some of us even evidence a furious hostility toward people whom we once dearly loved. Others, however, do succeed in concealing hostility by becoming almost wooden and formal. Some of us forsake our former patterns of social interaction. We cannot initiate an activity, even though we are eager to be active. We become restless and cannot sleep. Finally, we may experience the ultimate in the grief reaction manifested by deep depression, severe tenseness, unwarranted insomnia, feelings of worthlessness, bitter self-accusation, and desire for chastisement. A person with these latter symptoms may be seriously in danger of self-destruction.

The appearance of these reactions should prompt us to seek the counsel and spiritual aid that will help us through our crisis, since most of these manifestations can, with proper treatment at the hands of a skilled person, be transformed into normal reactions in which the patient will find proper resolutions.

YOU CAN DO MORE THAN SURVIVE.

RELIGION AND GRIEF

In a large measure, our religious faith will influence the way in which we will meet bereavement. Because sorrow is a spiritual pilgrimage, religion has attempted throughout the ages to give us comfort, courage, and hope for the experience. Our faith will do much to determine how the traumatic experience of bereavement will affect us. Religion deals with the meaning of life and death. Our spiritual faith has something to say about death, for religion alone provides us with the only hope for reunion with our departed loved ones.

> **A PERSON WITHOUT FAITH HAS A GREATER HANDICAP THAN ONE WITHOUT FEET.**

The pages of religious literature are replete with the testimonies of those who have found a new relationship with God through their grief. Such an awakening can be ours. What we believe about the future, and how we anticipate a spiritual reunion with the departed, will determine the way we face up to sorrow and death. Those of us who have faith in God will find the mystery of death less perplexing because we believe that all of life and death are in the hands of God; this includes a belief in immortality and the conviction that we will someday be reunited with our loved ones.

Some of us for the first time come to a meaningful understanding of God through the death of a loved one. Our loss may leave an aching emptiness that will draw us to God, whom we thought we could do without. There are some who "turn to religion" to ease their grief, as though faith were some sort of soothing syrup or emotional anesthetic. This is a perversion of religion. Nor should we look upon religion as a means of safeguarding us from trouble. No matter how spiritual we may be, we share with the rest of humanity the ills common to life in our world. Just because we trust in God does not imply that we will never lose our loved ones or our health, or that we shall never be disappointed or frustrated.

Religion will not be of much value if we have never been "over the road" before. Unless we are well practiced in its techniques, we may be too numb for it to be of much help. We must know how and where to go to find what we need. To be of real value in a grief experience, religion must be an integral part of our living – a way of life not merely a blanket that we wrap around our grief. Any attempt to ride "piggy-back" on religion as we pass through our experience of sorrow will be as frustrating and unrewarding as attempting to trap quicksilver. However, religion in the life of one who has had experience in it can be a strong support in the time of sorrow; it can provide a light in the darkness of our disillusionment and despair; it can provide us with a source of power beyond human resources that will enable us to resolve a tragedy into a triumph and our sorrow into a sacrament.

Normally we express our sorrow outwardly toward our friends, our loved ones, the world around us, and inwardly toward ourselves. It would seem that those who evidence the "faith that overcomes the world" give to their grief also an upward expression, which has something to do with God, and they want God to have something to do with them. At a time like this we can sense the presence of God, as real and vital as breathing, and nearer than hands and feet. We will never know what it really means to walk with God in the deepest sense until we have walked with Him in the dark. Any agonizing experience, if taken in stride with a loving Father's aid, will do something creative for us. The seeds of our sorrow will yield us a golden harvest of divine blessings when planted in the soil of faithful, believing hearts.

God is the source of power and provides us with strength for any situation. Most of us live in the narrow world of "self," and have not learned to cope with the difficult situations occurring in our lives. But when our world is centered in God, we come to know the "peace that passeth all understanding"; and we comprehend the meaning of the words, "Underneath are the everlasting arms." Grief does not need to be lonesome torture. We are not alone. This experience can be guided and utilized for a spiritual result. If we make use of the most wonderful of all stage directions, "Enter God," He will come into our experience and reveal His presence in a way beyond our power to describe. We, with God, can work this thing out together, for He will neither leave us nor forsake us in our darkest hour. "When through the deep waters thy trials shall lie, I will be with thee." Only when we come to the end of "self," will be really come to depend upon God. And He can be depended upon!

God is always with us, "Whither shall I go from thy Spirit?" (Psalm 139:7); "God is our refuge and strength, a very present help in trouble." (Psalm 46:1); "As a father pitieth his children, so the Lord pitieth them that fear him." (Psalm 103:13); "As one whom his mother comforteth, so will I comfort you." (Isaiah 66:13). Those of us who are parents are unceasingly solicitous of the comfort and well being of our children, and especially so when a child is suffering some hurt. God, as our Father, has something for us in our grief, but He will have more for us if we came to know Him as a loving Father before the experience of grief came to us. Many of us are in accord with the Psalmist's expression of real faith when he said, "What time I am afraid, I will trust in thee." (Psalm 56:3). But Isaiah gave evidence of a more mature and creative faith in the words, "Behold, God is my salvation; I will trust and not be afraid." (Isaiah 12:2). Isaiah's faith represents a step beyond the faith of the Psalmist.

Religion is something for us to use, not lose, during our time of bereavement. Because real and powerful sustaining comfort is one of the end products of faith, we may feel that our expression of grief betrays our lack of faith. Belief in immortality does not necessarily guarantee that we can control our grief and sublimate our sorrow. We who have faith in life everlasting are not being untrue to our faith when we permit our real feelings of loss to find expression. Faith in life everlasting does not deny in any way the deep sense of loss we suffer when we lose a loved one. No religion denies that separation is painful. To mourn is legitimate and consistent with the Christian faith as long as we do not mourn excessively and hopelessly as those "who have no hope." The Christian religion justifies mourning. Our expression of grief is no indication of our lack of faith. Even our Lord wept at the tomb of His good friend Lazarus. Our religion should not be looked upon as a substitute for grief or as an instrument to suppress it. Instead, our religion gives us the power and strength to meet grief head on, to pass through it, to rise above it, and to be strengthened by it.

Faith is not a means of short-circuiting grief; faith has the power to take our sorrow and transmute it into character and achievement. This is the very essence of the Christian faith. Our faith provides us the power by which we may be able to transform all experiences whether good, bad, or indifferent into the precious metal of Christ-like character. Faith is a divine alchemy that makes these elements yield a depth of maturity and Christ-likeness. Faith makes all things, good and bad, work together for the spiritual good of all who love God. "We know that in everything God works for good with those who love him, who are called according to his purpose." (Romans 8:28). Our religion teaches us how to bear sorrow, and in it we find the strength that will enable us to endure it in a worthy manner.

Almost all religions offer well-developed sacramental techniques to help us meet the challenge and advent of death and to veil the end of life with a halo of sacred solemnity. Maybe this is the reason why the older minister's manuals refer to the funeral as a "holy celebration." In addition to serving as expressions of faith, the rituals of religion for the dead provide us with the opportunity for a healthy, cleansing release of emotions. Through dogma, ritual, and sincere personal interest, our religion helps us to accept the pain of loss, maintain our contact with the living, and overcome our morbid guilt feelings through the medium of divine grace. In a very real and effective way, our religion performs its most heroic feat as we stand beside the grave.

We may not come to the true understanding of Christ's words, "Blessed are they that mourn for they shall be comforted," until we ourselves have actually mourned. Not until we are faced with the reality of loss can we fully accept His comfort, feel His presence and help, and know that He holds our hand.

There are times when we might feel that in taking our loved one away God is punishing us. The idea that tragedy, sorrow, and suffering are the result of and the price for sin comes from the pronouncements of some whose experiences are recorded in the Old Testament of our Bible. Our New Testament is not in accord with such precepts. On several occasions, Jesus corrected those who questioned Him regarding retribution. Luke 13:1-5 records the following incident: "There were present at that season some that told him of the Galileans, whose blood Pilate had mingled with their sacrifices [apparently they were innocent victims]; and Jesus answering said unto them, Suppose ye that these Galileans were sinners above all the Galileans, because they suffered these things? I tell you, No. Or those eighteen upon whom the tower of Siloam fell, and slew them, think ye that they were sinners above all men that dwelt in Jerusalem? I tell you, No!" John 9:2-3 relates a similar response of our Lord when the disciples noticed a man blind from birth, "and his disciples asked him saying, Master, who did sin, this man, or his parents, that he was born blind? Jesus answered, Neither hath this man sinned, nor his parents."

The Bible can be a source of great strength and comfort to us in the time of sorrow. There are many passages that express the feelings and the faith of others who have also passed through the valley of weeping. A careful reading and study of these verses will enable us to make firmer the foundation of our faith in the ongoing purposes of God in our own lives and in the lives of our loved ones who have preceded us. We can find most helpful the following passages in the Old Testament: Deuteronomy 33:27; Joshua 1:9; II Samuel 12:18-23; Psalm 23; 27:1-10; 42:1-4; 46; 91; 121; Isaiah 25:8-9; 26:3; 40:28-31; 43:2. In the New Testament we can turn to Matthew 5:4; 11:28; John 11:25-26; 14:1-11, 18-21; 16:33; Romans 5:1-5; 8:38-39; 14:7-8; I Corinthians 15:20-28, 35-50, 53-58; II Corinthians 1:3-5; 4:13-14, 16-18; 5:1-8; Philippians 4:13; I Thessalonians 4:13-14; II Timothy 1:8-10; Revelation 21:1-7.

As we read the Bible passages that refer to death, we become aware of the fact that the writers did not always call it death. They used expressions alive with beautiful meanings. The Psalmist spoke of passing "though the valley of the shadow of death that I might dwell in the house of the Lord"; Jesus spoke of dying as entering the Father's house of many mansions; Paul referred to death as putting off this tabernacle (tent) of clay that he might be clothed upon with an "eternal" garment; Peter spoke of death as an "entrance ministered abundantly," a great open door at the top of the roadway of life.

Why did they speak of death with words like these? We frequently employ figures of speech and euphemisms to lessen the emotional shock of the real meaning of a word or the experience it describes. In other words, we are afraid of it. The Biblical writers used euphemistic expressions for a very different reason – they were not afraid of death. They saw the other side of the phenomenon, for they possessed the instrument of faith which enabled them to understand death. Their experiences were much like ours as we look at ordinary sunlight through a glass prism. To our physical eye, unaided, sunlight appears plain, colorless, and ordinary, but when we view it through a prism, it reveals all the colors of the rainbow because sunlight is a composite of all the rainbow colors. Just as the prism helps our physical eye distinguish the radiant band of colors, so does the instrument of faith help us to understand death and bereavement.

As a people whose religious faith rests on the resurrection of Jesus Christ, we profess to believe in the resurrection and life everlasting. This doctrine teaches us that death is not the end but is only a transition to another room in our Father's house. Our loved ones are not lost; rather, they have only gone before us. For them the experience is one of gain rather than of loss. They have been loosed and freed from the limitations of the flesh. They are "absent from the body and present with the Lord" (II Corinthians 5:8).

We may be tempted to dwell so long upon our own sense of loss that we completely lose sight of the experience of the one who has died. George MacDonald in *THE HIDDEN LIFE* calls our attention to the fact that "death has two sides to it – one sunny and one dark, as this round world of ours is every day half sunny and half dark. We on the dark side call the mystery death; while they on the other, looking down in glad light, await the glad birth with other tears than ours." Our Christian faith makes death "glorious and triumphant for through its portals we enter into the presence of the living God."

The following story of "The Ship" has appeared in so very many versions and over so very many different names that today no one is really sure who wrote it the first time. It illustrates well the matter we are concerned with.

I am standing on the seashore. A ship at my side spreads her white sails to the morning breeze and starts for the blue ocean. She is an object of beauty and strength, and I stand and watch her until she is only a ribbon of white cloud just where the sea and sky come to mingle with each other. Then someone at my side says, "There, she's gone." "Gone where?" Gone from my sight, that is all. She is just as large in mast and hull and spar as she was when she left my side, and just as able to bear her load of living freight to the place of destination. Her diminished size is in me, not in her; and just at the moment when someone at my side says, "There, she's gone," there are other voices ready to take up the glad shout: "There – she comes." And that is dying.

> **LIFE'S ROAD IS ROUGH, BUT YOU CAN MAKE IT.
> HOLD OUT YOUR HAND AND GOD WILL TAKE IT.**

Even though we may profess a faith in the verities of the Christian religion, we may not always succeed in allowing these beliefs to guide our lives and our actions. Once a woman who professed to be a Christian stood at the open grave of her husband. Suddenly she screamed with uncontrolled and thoughtless emotion and no one could comfort her. A woman who knew her turned away in disgust, muttering, "Poor soul, I thought she believed it." People do watch us. They can tell whether our faith is only slushy sentiment that will melt under the dripping of tears or whether our confidence in God is the sort that will weather any storm.

From the past comes the story of a church school superintendent and his wife who, on Good Friday, had buried their two daughters who had died of diphtheria. Probably no one in their fellowship expected them to be at their customary posts at the church on Easter Sunday; but they were there. The superintendent led the hymns with choking voice, and his wife taught her class despite her tears. Following the service a lad, walking home with his father, remarked, "Dad, they sure believe it, don't they?" "Believe what?" the father inquired. "Oh, all this about Easter and eternal life." The father answered, "Of course, all Christians believe that." The boy replied, "I know, but they don't believe it like that."

When we lose our loved ones, we may be tempted to ask, "Why?" This may lead to tragic bitterness of soul. The clenched-fist method of dealing with our sorrow will make us tense and rebellious so that the healing, peace-giving power of God will not be able to get through to us. We may never understand the reason why our loved one was taken from us, but the fact that God had a reason should comfort us and is better than if we were able to find a dozen reasons. We spoke earlier of God's perfect will and His permissive will. Many experiences may come to us, His children, which He permits but has not ordered. This is what we mean by God's permissive will. Although we recognize the dangers inherent in seeking the "Why" of death, we also need to remember that at no time in our lives do we ever come closer to our Lord than when we ask, "Why?" Let us not forget that from His cross on the afternoon that He died, our Lord asked, "Father, why hast though forsaken me?"

> ### ACCEPTANCE OF WHAT HAS HAPPENED
> ### IS THE FIRST STEP TO OVERCOMING
> ### THE CONSEQUENCES OF ANY MISFORTUNE.
> *William James*

In the past, the word "submission" was often used by some churchmen when they referred to the sorrows of life. Perhaps this connotation was unfortunate, for submission suggests a picture of one bowed down and crushed like a slave beneath the whip of his master. Today, we have a more positive word, "acceptance." When we accept something, we acknowledge its presence, and in so doing we find comfort and peace. Perhaps acceptance was in the mind of our Lord when He said in the presence of disappointment, "Even so, Father, for so it seemed good in thy sight" (Matthew 11:26). Here we have the key to the whole matter. If we are able to accept life's difficult experiences and remain at peace in our minds, it may be that the greater part of the victory will already have been won.

In conclusion, may we suggest that we surrender ourselves and our sorrows to the healing hands of God. If we will, we shall discover that God will provide healing if we but give Him the opportunity – but we must give Him that chance. It would be easy for God to spare a life, but He performs a greater miracle when He changes our life attitude. When what seems to be a tragedy actually becomes a triumph, and when what is a farewell rite becomes a coronation, God has performed His great miracle of spiritual healing. We should thank Him for the experience even though we do not understand.

NON-ACCEPTANCE DOES NOT CHANGE THE FACT OF WHAT HAS HAPPENED.

We may never come to the place in our lives when the sense of bereavement will completely cease to be. God does not so promise. He promises us joy for the morning, and the Scriptures assure us that only in the great beyond will God wipe all our tears away. As long as mortal life lasts, we can avail ourselves of the comforting ministry of God through His Spirit. In Him there is grace to bind up our wounds and to heal our broken hearts. He will provide strength to undergird us lest we plunge into the abyss of despair. From Him comes the power that enables us to get back bravely into the stream of normal life again and assume our obligations with new vigor and resolve. "This is the victory that overcomes the world – even our faith." (I John 5:4)

WHAT YOU CANNOT CHANGE YOU MIGHT AS WELL ACCEPT.

THE PATHWAY

(Applies especially to the

A. SHOCK

Numbness; disorder; panic; denial; like being in a trance; crying. (This is temporary – may last for hours, days, weeks.)

B. ACUTE STAGE – The suffering of grieving – These occur in no specific order – some not at all.

Anxiety episodes; mental pain; "I'm losing my mind"; frustration; sadness; fear; bitterness; insecurity; anger; irritability; crying; depression; helplessness; yearning and searching for the lost person; emptiness; "If only"; feeling isolated from others; difficulty in concentrating; guilt; hostility; self-pity; resentment toward others; inability to think clearly; confusion; **L O N E L I N E S S**; lack of awareness and judgment; blaming God; "Why me?"; loss of patterns of conduct; inability to accept reality; fatigue; hopelessness; heartache; visual and auditory proof that the loved one still lives and will return; withdrawal from others; fear of the future; inability to return to normal activities; bewilderment and much more!

LOWEST or TURNING POINT (not everyone's experience)

The choice we make: UP or DOWN

Resigning yourself to "poor me";
Chronic depression;
Anger towards self and others;
Physical, mental and emotional illness;
Low life satisfaction;
Unhappiness;
NO REAL RECOVERY!

THE PATHWAY

THROUGH GRIEF
Widowed and/or Divorced)

C. **READJUSTMENT** – recovery, resolution, acceptance – (one to two years or more from time of loss is normal.)
Getting on with living;
Reorganizing your life;
Renewed sense of well being;
Completing the grief work;
Discovering your independence;
Following up on dormant interests;
Building self-esteem: the cycle-self examination produces self knowledge, which can beget self-esteem, which is necessary for self-confidence;
Setting and attaining new goals;
Trying new life patterns;
Forming new friendships and associations;
Joining support group;
Establishing new identity – self-worth;
Reassessing how things are now;
Accepting your new role as a "single";
"I will work my way through this!";
Accepting responsibility for yourself.

The circles in the path represent relapses into acute grieving brought on by an occurrence related to the memory of the loved one. They are periods when we regress and make no progress. They decrease in frequency and intensity as the grief work continues.

****

This chart is adapted and modified from another source (authorship unknown) by the author.

THE PATHWAY THROUGH GRIEF
(Applies Especially to the Widowed and/or Divorced)

A prominent doctor who treats cancer patients in one of our local hospitals recently made this statement in a newspaper interview: "People who are terminally ill or who have had radical surgery need to learn how to live with their illness, and I make it a point to apprise them of what they can expect down the road". That's telling it like it is, and in most cases this might be the best approach. However, because we are all different and each one of us has our own way of handling the crises of life, it might not be the wisest course for each patient. Some doctors even go so far as to tell a patient how long they may expect to live. In my opinion, no doctor should do this; it might become a self-fulfilling prophecy.

Some patients would be so devastated by his prophecy of the course of their illness that they wouldn't even try to cooperate with his treatment. They might just give up, lie down and await the sweet messenger of death. If the patient really wants to know how long he/she might live, the doctor might say as a challenge; "That pretty much depends upon you. If you have the courage and strength to fight this disease, you just might win many more years for yourself."

There are countless instances on record of patients who made it their mission to beat the doctor's odds. They realize that his M.D. signifies that he is a doctor of medicine and not a minor deity. Thousands of people have lived many years beyond extreme and violent surgical procedures. An increasingly large number of cancer patients experience remission and live out their normal lifespan – they simply refuse to die on a doctor's order.

The experience of losing a loved one by death or divorce is very much like that of a recovery from surgery or illness. It's a long, arduous task, filled with hard work and diligence. Most people eventually recover from bereavement. They may never really get over it, but they do get through it, and so can you.

That's what this *PATHWAY THROUGH GRIEF* (see Chart on pages 68-69) is all about. It tries to show you what is down the road, so you won't complain: "Why didn't someone tell me it was going to be like this?" This is no timetable for grieving, nor does it guarantee that if you start from Point A and touch all the bases through Point C (readjustment on the top right of the chart), you will have won the battle and your grief will be healed. It doesn't happen that way because the pathway through grief is not lineal, but zig-zagged. There is no steady progression from grief to non-grief. There are peaks and valleys. Because each of us is different, we make our own timetable in dealing with the experience.

I'm not very comfortable with suggesting that there are stages in the grieving process. I do believe we can be aware that there are at least three basic and noticeable points involved: A. SHOCK; B. ACUTE STAGE, suffering; and finally C. READJUSTMENT, or acceptance, or recovery. Just as in a surgical procedure, there is the shock of the experience during which the patient may be little aware of what is going on. When consciousness returns, there is pain and suffering, and finally recovery. As we recuperate from accidents, surgery or illness, so we recover from the other traumas of life; including the worst of all, the loss of a loved one.

Recovery seldom comes by miracle, but rather by slow, torturous, painful plodding. That seems to be nature's way. You will never get over it, but you can get through it. Eventually the wound will close and there will be a scar, beneath which lies the marvel of healing that took place. Scars may not be nice to look at, but the only alternative to a scar is a chronic, open wound. Of course, there is some comfort to be gained in knowing that there are stages. The term infers that eventually there will be a final stage beyond which you will be able to get on with your life, which may seem a long way from where you are right now.

> **PATHWAYS ARE FOR WALKING ON.**
> **THEY LEAD FROM ONE PLACE TO ANOTHER.**

A. SHOCK

When someone told you that your loved one had died, you crash-landed into a whole new world which you never expected to see or experience. Everything seemed upside down, inside out, unreal, as though your whole world had come to an end. You were in a state of shock. There was numbness, disorder, panic, inability to believe it had really happened. You told yourself, "I'm dreaming and some day I will wake up and find this isn't real." It was like being in a trance; tears came uncontrolled; it was utter despair. Perhaps others had to do for you what you could not do for yourself: what funeral home to call, plans to be made for a service, purchasing a cemetery plot, etc. – this while you were almost totally unaware of what was going on – too stricken to function.

Unfortunately, too often tranquilizing drugs are administered to a person going through this experience in the belief that it will help them. Ironically, many felt later on that they had been cheated rather than spared. There is some truth to the saying, "You must feel if you are going to heal." The use of drugs can prevent the grief work from being carried out. In a situation of this nature, it is more therapeutic to be a participant rather than a desensitized spectator. Most of us would profit more by being awake and conscious through it all. In some ways this state of seeming unconsciousness, which is a part of the shock experience, is both a mercy and a blessing. It's very much like the effect of a severe injury or disease which results in such excruciating pain which, if it were not turned off into unconsciousness, would be fatal.

The only mourners who may be spared the experience of shock are those whose loved one passed away following a lengthy illness. For weeks or months they may have been dealing with anticipatory grief and will have already travelled part of the pathway. However, very few people are really prepared for the death of a loved one no matter how long they may have anticipated it. When it finally does happen, they are almost as emotionally devastated as if they had no warning.

The state of shock may last for a matter of hours; for some, it may be days before the real nature of things begin to appear. Unfortunately there are others for whom this tragic condition may continue for several months. For many, it may re-occur in the months that follow.

Down the left side of the chart, you will notice circles which are spaced intermittently along the way. I think most of us would agree that grief is cruel. Why doesn't it hit us just once and then go away and leave us alone to heal? Every novice in this fellowship of suffering knows that it doesn't work this way. It keeps coming back to hit us again.

You may be congratulating yourself on your recent progress; you haven't felt the need to go to the cemetery for the past week. In general, things seem to be on the upgrade and you're feeling good about your progress. Then something unexpected and dreadful happens: a personal letter addressed to your love one is delivered, sent by someone who didn't know about the death, or you accidentally come across some special memento charged with deep feelings for your loved one, or someone makes a remark which opens the wound. Suddenly, and without warning, you are back into the despair of acute grieving. All your progress seems to have vanished. Heartbreak and dismay take the field. How disheartening and upsetting! You think to yourself, "I went forward three steps and then fell back two. I'll never get through this."

> **MOST PEOPLE IN THE ACUTE STAGE OF GRIEVING ARE NOT HIGHLY MOTIVATED TO DO ANYTHING.**

These relapses into painful grieving and going around in a circle of self-pity are normal to most people travelling this road and you are not to blame yourself for having temporarily backslid. You didn't cause it. What brought it on was a heavy blow which struck you on a very sore spot which was trying to heal. These relapses may last for a matter of minutes, hours, or may even spoil the bigger part of a week for you. Eventually you will pick yourself up and get back on the road again. Remember, this is normal.

The best thing to do when a relapse occurs is to attack the course by taking the offensive; go to lunch with someone, go shopping, get out of the house for awhile (even leave town), have a good cry, make it a real pity party, help someone who needs you. You will find that when you help someone out of a hole (depression, problem, difficulty, etc.), you will have, without even trying, buried some of your own problems in that hole. This is a miracle. But God does not perform it. He has reserved it for you. Only you can do it. Dry your tears and begin to count your blessings instead of your burdens.

There is good news. Notice that the circles (relapses) drawn into the pathway at the beginning are boldly outlined and occur more frequently in the early stages. As you move along they become farther apart and less intense in their impact. Eventually they will disappear. Don't be disheartened if you experience one or more in the second or third year of your loss.

B. THE ACUTE STAGE – Suffering

Just as in the experience following surgery, after unconsciousness and numbness wear off, pain and suffering set in. Notice the long list of negative emotional experiences listed in this section. As a grieving person, you are a candidate for any one or combination of them. What a collection of impressive and frightening negatives! What an emotional mob scene – a real patch of weeds! The picture of grief is painted in many colors, most of them somber and dark. Many of these emotions you have already experienced; hopefully some of them will not be yours. They appear in no special order. All of them, within reasonable limits, are normal. You are not losing your mind. Notice also that loneliness is highlighted because it is the most common experience of people who have lost a significant loved one.

Some problems we meet in life are insolvable, but they can be made manageable. That is what a grief support group is all about; we can learn to cope. Falling into water does not drown a person, but staying there without fighting back ends in drowning. When you choose to act, you become an agent of life rather than a victim of it. Right now, the place of readjustment seems so far away that it might as well not exist. It's a vague dream, a figment of the imagination. Someday you may find it by doing your grief work and then realize that it was more than a dream. There is help for your grief; most of it is at the end of your arm. You have to work it out yourself. John James in *THE GRIEF RECOVERY HANDBOOK* says, "No book or counselor or friend or support group can recover you from grief. Only you can recover yourself."

GRIEF IS NOT GOING TO GO AWAY BY ITSELF; YOU HAVE TO WORK AT IT.

Whatever the variety of emotions we experience, if we try to understand them and realize that they are normal, we may learn how to cope with them.

Notice about two-thirds of the way down the left side of the chart the LOWEST or TURNING point. For some very fortunate people this point is not in their itinerary. They never have to make the decision about whether they will go on and work their way through it because they have always met the crises of life in positive and practical ways. They have learned how to accept the unacceptable and surmount the insurmountable. They are the well-adjusted ones, and definitely a minority. They and all who know them realize that they will make it because they have developed a positive response to all the difficulties of life. No one worries about them. This does not mean they do not grieve, because they do. They have learned how to deal constructively with whatever life hands them – a rare breed to be sure.

In order for a turning point to occur, someone or something has to change. This happened to Mary Ellen, as she shared the experiences of her widowhood with a group. "One day I just sat down and made up my mind. I decided he is not here, but I am; he is dead but I am alive; so I'm going to do whatever I can to get on with my life. That's why I joined this support group." And she did get on with her life.

What you do or don't do about your grief depends on you. It's not a can or cannot situation, but rather a will or will not proposition. This can be the most challenging undertaking of your whole life; you need to make the decision to go on.

During much of the time up to this point, the grieving person has been in what a parachutist would call a "free-fall", with no control. The only direction is down. But once the parachute has opened, there is an element

of control. The experienced parachutist can, at least part-
ly, direct and guide the descent and land on the target, and
so can you.

A person may be in a "free-fall" for weeks or months
with no apparent direction or control, and then one day
make the decision, "I'm going to work my way through
this." Now the parachute is open, and this marks a turning point, a new direction, and a new experience.

Not every grieving person comes to this decision or
turning point. They drift along like a tumbleweed in the
desert, being pushed around by every passing wind (the
emotions of suffering). They have no motivating power
within them to control their direction. They shut out the
world, pull the covers over their heads, and dwell on
yesterdays and what used to be. They never make the turn
into the upward path toward recovery. They continue on
a downward spiral; they will not learn how to fight back.
For the rest of their life, they continue in their grief with
NO REAL RECOVERY. I'm sure you know someone
who fits this category.

C. READJUSTMENT

Even though we don't normally think of mourning as
a process of recovery, there can be no recovery without it.
Every person who consciously or unconsciously decides,
"I will work my way through this," moves on to the other
side and begins the upward climb. Sadness begins to sub-
side; memories are easier to live with, become even
pleasant; you can even laugh again, and resume normal activities. It sounds easy, but it isn't. There just is no simple,
easy way through grief; it's a long, hard, painful and
repetitive climb. The dividends are compounded daily.

It's worth it! After all, what is the alternative? NO REAL RECOVERY.

I assure you that if I could tear off two years from the calendar and transplant you to that point, you would feel different and better since so many things will have changed. Accept your new role as a "single" if you lost your mate. Establish a new identity and self-worth. Reach out by forming new friendships and interests. Experiment with new life patterns. Set new goals. Do some things you've always wanted to do. Follow up some long-suppressed interests. Complete your grief work. Join a support group. Many studies indicate that if we have a focus outside ourselves, it will help us survive the crises of life.

Instead of allowing your thoughts to be directed inwardly in self-pity, volunteer your services to help others who are less fortunate than you are, or to the many causes which depend on volunteers to keep them going.

Build a new self-esteem. The equation goes like this: self-examination produces self-knowledge, which can beget self-esteem, which is necessary for self-confidence. Readjustment will come. Grief work hurts, but it works, it's painful but it pays.

While you may grieve because of a loss, you can keep yourself from losing the perspective and appreciation for the many good things that can still happen in your life. It was Helen Keller who said, "When one door closes, another opens, but often we look so long at the closed door that we do not see the one which has opened for us."

You can do more than survive. You can emerge as a better person if you will really work at it. The worst thing you can do now is to do nothing.

Comparatively speaking, there are not many things in this world which are impossible. According to the older laws of aerodynamics, the bumblebee cannot fly because its fuselage is too big for its wing area. Fortunately, the bumblebee doesn't know this; he just flies.

I have the confidence that you will never meet anything you can't handle. You may not believe this now, but if you will apply all the resources at your disposal, including those within yourself, you will discover it. Courage isn't having the strength to go on; it's going on when you don't have the strength.

How long does all this take? It all depends on how well and completely you work on it. The route one takes on the pathway does not depend on CAN or CANNOT, but on WILL or WILL NOT.

You are now faced with the most demanding undertaking of your life. Any good that may come to you in the future will depend more on you than on anyone else. If you are willing to work your way, there can be an end to sorrow and your life can go on and be meaningful again. It is not what happens to you but what you do about it that determines the outcome. Happiness depends more on ourselves than on the circumstances of our lives. You cannot control what comes to you, but you can decide what you will do about it. You will never get over it, but you CAN get through it. Commit yourself to life.

> **IF IT'S GOING TO BE**
> **IT'S UP TO ME.**

ALL IS WELL

The Lord may not have planned that this should overtake me, but He has most certainly permitted it. Therefore, though it were an attack of the enemy, by the time it reaches me, it has the Lord's permission, and therefore all is well. He will make it work together with all life's experiences for good.

Author unknown

We know that all things work together for good to them that love God.

Romans 8:28

THE FALLEN WALLS

It was a dwelling place no more,
Of one we loved who lived within a while;
We knew his presence by his deeds;
We knew his nearness by his smile.

It was the instrument by which he worked;
They were his hands, his feet,
Muscle and bone and nerve he used
To make his tale of years complete.

But dwellings crumble with the years;
Walls totter, timbers rot;
The tool from constant years wears out and fails;
This is our common lot.

We call it death, and dread the parting hour
When the loved form at last is laid away.
We dread the tender rites that mark
The disposition of the common clay.

But lo! A greater truth we know;
Tho now the tenant dwells within no more;
He only moved away; he gained
Translation to a fairer shore.

Life ended to begin anew;
Beyond our sight he liveth still.
We can but dream of what he knows;
We can but trust our Father's will.

And trusting turn to common tasks,
Dreaming the while of life beyond the years.
God's perfect love holds him and us,
And God Himself shall wipe away all tears.

Author unknown

LIFE'S WEAVING

My life is but a weaving
  Between my God and me.
I cannot choose the colors;
  He knows what they should be.

Ofttimes He weaveth sorrow.
  Which seemeth strange to me.
But I shall trust His judgment
  And work on faithfully.

'Tis He who fills the shuttle;
  He knows just what is best;
So I shall trust His judgment
  And leave with Him the rest.

The dark threads are as needful
  In the weaver's skillful hand
As the threads of gold and silver
  In the pattern He has planned.

Not till the loom is silent
  And the shuttles cease to fly
Shall God unroll the canvass
  And explain the reason why.

At last when life is over
  With Him I shall abide;
Then I shall view the pattern
  Upon the upper side.

Then I shall know the reason
Why pain with joy entwined
Was woven in the fabric
Of a life that God designed.

Author unknown

FOOTPRINTS

One night a man had a dream and in his dream he reviewed the footsteps he had taken in his life.

He looked and noticed that all over the mountains and difficult places that he had traveled there was one set of footprints; but over the plains and down the hills, there were two sets of footprints, as if someone had walked by his side.

He turned to Christ and said, "There is something I don't understand. Why is it that down the hills and over the smooth and easy places you have walked by my side, but here over the tough and difficult places I have walked alone, for I see in those areas there is just one set of footprints?"

Christ turned to the man and said, "It is that while your life was easy I walked by your side; but here, where the walking was hard and the paths were difficult, was the time you needed Me most, and that is why I carried you."

Author unknown.

OTHER HELPFUL READING

For the Widowed:

Caine, Lynn. *LIFELINES*. Garden City, NY: Doubleday & Co., 1978.

Campbell, Scott and Silverman, Phyllis, *WIDOWER*. New York: Prentice-Hall, 1987.

Fisher, Ida and Lane, Byron. *THE WIDOW'S GUIDE TO LIFE*. Long Beach, CA: Lane-Con Press, 1985.

Grollman, Earl A. *LIVING WHEN A LOVED ONE HAS DIED*. Boston: Beacon Press, 1977.

Ginsburg, Genevieve Davis. *TO LIVE AGAIN*. Los Angeles: Jeremy P. Tarcher, 1987.

Kohn, Jane B. and Willard K. *THE WIDOWER*. Boston: Beacon Press, 1976.

Kushner, Harold S. *WHEN BAD THINGS HAPPEN TO GOOD PEOPLE*. New York: Avon Books, 1981.

Marshall, Catherine. TO LIVE AGAIN. New York: McGraw Hill, 1957.

Miller, Yolanda. *YOU CAN BECOME WHOLE AGAIN*. Atlanta: John Knox Press, 1981.

Morris, Sarah. *GRIEF AND HOW TO LIVE WITH IT*. New York: Grossett & Dunlap.

Nudel, Adele Rice. *STARTING OVER. Help For Young Widows and Widowers.* New York: Dodd Mead, 1986.

Nye, Miriam. *BUT I NEVER THOUGHT HE'D DIE.* Philadelphia: Westminster Press, 1978.

Silverman, William B. and Cinnamon, Kenneth M. *WHEN MOURNING COMES.* Chicago: Nelson-Hall, 1982.

Start, Clarissa. *WHEN YOU'RE A WIDOW.* St. Louis: Concordia, 1968.

Stearns, Ann Kaiser. *LIVING THROUGH PERSONAL CRISIS.* Chicago: The Thomas Moore Press, 1984.

Veninga, Robert L. *A GIFT OF HOPE. How We Survive Our Tragedies.* New York: Ballantine Books, 1985.

Wylie, Betty Jane. *THE SURVIVAL GUIDE FOR WIDOWS.* New York: Ballantine Books, 1982.

For the Divorced:

Krantzler, Mel. *CREATIVE DIVORCE.* New York: M. Evans and Co., 1973.

Krantzler, Mel. *LEARNING TO LOVE AGAIN.* New York: Thomas W. Crowell Co., Inc., 1977.

Smoke, Jim. *GROWING THROUGH DIVORCE.* Irvine, CA: Harvest House Publishing Co., 1976.

Young, Amy Ross. *BY DEATH OR DIVORCE. It Hurts To Lose.* Denver: Accent Books, 1976.

For Parents Whose Child Has Died:

Donnelly, Katherine S. *RECOVERING FROM THE LOSS OF A CHILD.* New York: Macmillan, 1982.

Fischoff, Joseph and Brohl, Noreen. *BEFORE AND AFTER MY CHILD DIED.* Detroit: Emmons-Fairfield, 1981.

Schiff, Harriett Sarnoff. *THE BEREAVED PARENT.* New York: Crown Publishers, Inc., 1977.

For Children Who Have Lost A Loved One:

Grollman, Earl A. *TALKING ABOUT DEATH – A Dialogue Between Parent and Child.* Boston: Beacon Press, 1976.

Jackson, Edgar N. *TELLING A CHILD ABOUT DEATH.* New York: Channel Press, 1965.

Schaefer, Dan and Lyons, Christine. *HOW DO WE TELL THE CHILDREN?* New York: Newmarket Press, 1986.

Vogel, Linda Jane. *HELPING A CHILD UNDER-STAND DEATH.* Philadelphia: Fortress Press, 1975.

For Survivors of Suicide:

Hewett, John. *AFTER SUICIDE.* Philadelphia: Westminster Press, 1973.

Ross, Elnora. *AFTER SUICIDE – A Unique Grief Process.* Springfield, Illinois, 1981.

For Those Who Have Experienced SIDS, Stillbirth, Miscarriage, Neo-natal Death:

Borg, Susan and Lasker, Judith. *WHEN PREGNANCY FAILS.* Boston: Beacon Press, 1981.

DeFrain, John. *STILLBORN – The Invisible Death.* Lexington, Massachusetts: Lexington Books, 1986.

Ilse, Sherokee and Burns, Linda. *MISCARRIAGE.* Long Lake, Minnesota: Wintergreen Press, 1985.

Vredevelt, Pam W. *EMPTY ARMS – Stillbirth.* Portland, OR: Multnomah Press, 1984.